OCT 1 4 2010

HAIL!
AZTECS

Jen Green

Crabtree Publishing Company

www.crabtreebooks.com

Crabtree Publishing Company

www.crabtreebooks.com

Author: Jen Green
Editor: Lynn Peppas
Project coordinator: Kathy Middleton
Production coordinator: Ken Wright
Prepress technician: Ken Wright
Managing editor: Miranda Smith
Designer: Lorna Phillips
Picture researcher: Clare Newman
Design manager: David Poole
Editorial director: Lindsey Lowe
Children's publisher: Anne O'Daly
Consultant: Dr Paul G. Bahn

Photographs:
Alamy: Travelpic: p. 12 (bottom)
Art Archive: p. 11 (bottom left); Bibliotea Nacional
   Madrid/Gianne Dagli Orti: p. 20 (bottom right);
   Templo Mayor Library, Mexico/Gianni Dagli Orti:
   p. 11 (top left), 14 (center right), 22 (bottom left),
   23 (top left); National Archives, Mexico/Gianni
   Dagli Orti: p. 22 (center right)
Bridgeman Art Library: Peter Newark American
   Archives: p. 11 (bottom right)
Clipart: p. 3 (bottom), 8 (bottom left), 15 (bottom
   right), 20 (bottom left), 24 (top left), 25 (center),
   28 (bottom right)

Corbis: Gianni Dagli Ori: p. 6 (top right), 7 (top left),
   9 (center left), 12 (center left), 13 (center right);
   Historical Picture Archive: p. 21 (bottom left);
   Charles & Josette Lenars: p. 13 (center left); Guido
   Manuilo/epa: p. 11 (top right); The Art Archive:
   p. 26 (bottom left); Werner Forman: p. 3 (top right),
   13 (bottom left), 15 (top left), 21 (top left)
iStockphoto: Stanislaff: p. 18 (bottom left), Ivonne
   Wiernk-Van Wetten: p. 27 (center left)
Jupiter Images: cover (left), p. 29 (center left)
Library of Congress: p. 10
Thinkstock: p. 5 (bottom right), 27 (bottom right),
   28 (top left)
Topham: Fotoware Fotostation: p. 20 (top right),
   Dallas & John Heaton: p. 12 (top left photo),
   The Granger Collection: p. 3 (center right), 5
   (bottom left), 7 (top right), 8 (top and bottom right),
   12 (center right), 16 (center right), 17 (center left),
   17 (bottom right); Ullstein Bild: p. 27 (top left)
Werner Forman: p. 16 (center left); St. Louis Art
   Museum: p. 9 (bottom left)
Other images by Shutterstock

The book was produced for Crabtree Publishing
Company by Brown Reference Group.

Library and Archives Canada Cataloguing in Publication

Green, Jen
   Hail! Aztecs / Jen Green.

(Hail! History)
Includes index.
ISBN 978-0-7787-6625-4 (bound).--ISBN 978-0-7787-6632-2 (pbk.)

   1. Aztecs--Juvenile literature. 2. Aztecs--Social life and
customs--Juvenile literature. I. Title. II. Title: Aztecs.
III. Series: Hail! History

F1219.73.G74 2010   j972'.018   C2010-901753-6

Library of Congress Cataloging-in-Publication Data

Green, Jen.
   Hail! Aztecs / Jen Green.
      p. cm. -- (Hail! History)
   Includes index.
   ISBN 978-0-7787-6625-4 (reinforced lib. bdg. : alk. paper) --
   ISBN 978-0-7787-6632-2 (pbk. : alk. paper)
   1. Aztecs--Juvenile literature. 2. Aztecs--Social life and customs--
Juvenile literature. I. Title. II. Series.

   F1219.73.G774 2010
   972'.01--dc22
                                                         2010009547

Crabtree Publishing Company
www.crabtreebooks.com   1-800-387-7650
Copyright © **2011 CRABTREE PUBLISHING COMPANY.**

Printed in China/072010/AP20100226

Published in Canada
Crabtree Publishing
616 Welland Ave.
St. Catharines, Ontario
L2M 5V6

Published in the United States
Crabtree Publishing
PMB 59051
350 Fifth Avenue, 59th Floor
New York, New York 10118

CONTENTS

YOUR GUIDE TO
THE AZTECS

Welcome to the amazing Aztec empire. You join us around 1500 CE, when our empire is at its height, and we are the strongest power in Central America. *HAIL!* guides you through the Aztec world, but it is a pretty dangerous place, so be careful...don't say you haven't been warned!

WHO ARE THE AZTECS?

We are newcomers in Mesoamerica (middle America). In 1100 CE, drought and famine drove us south. We wandered for 150 years until our god, Huitzilopochtli, showed us where to settle—Lake Texcoco in the valley of Mexico. We call ourselves Mexica.

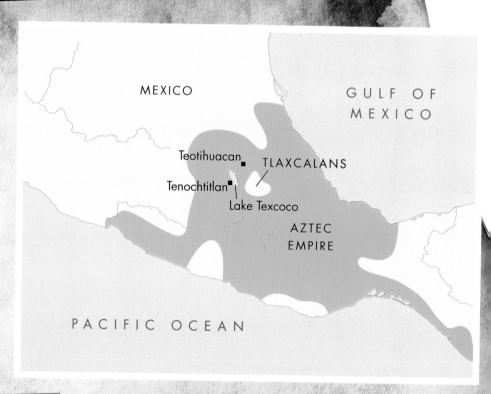

DON'T CONFUSE US WITH...
Olmecs, Mayans, or Toltecs

✪ The **OLMECS** were the original top dogs. They ruled from 1200 BCE, carved giant stone heads, then mysteriously vanished around 400 BCE.

✪ The **MAYANS** founded an empire to the east about 500 CE. They are still around now and are brilliant at math and building pyramid temples.

✪ The **TOLTECS** ruled the area around our capital city from 450 to 1200 CE. We took over from them and have many of the same gods.

HAIL! QUIZ WHY ARE THE AZTECS FAMOUS?

Take part in our readers' poll to find out why the Aztecs are so famous.

1. ISLAND CAPITAL
Our capital city, Tenochtitlan, is built on an island in a lake. It is surrounded by "floating fields" where we grow all our food. It is an extraordinary place, as you will find out when you visit.

2. WAR AND WARRIORS
No doubt about it, Aztecs are a bloodthirsty bunch. We are always at war with our neighbors as we strive to gain wealth and territory. Our warriors are the fiercest in the world.

3. HUMAN SACRIFICE
I'm afraid it is true—we do sacrifice humans, and it happens daily, not just every now and then. On special occasions, we sacrifice thousands of captives. And yes, we do eat people—only the best parts, though!

4. LAW AND ORDER
The Aztec empire is famed for its tough laws. Aztecs are sticklers for the rules and have harsh punishments for anyone who breaks them. The higher the rank, the worse the punishment!

5. AGRICULTURE
We cultivate any land that we can, draining swamps and using new systems to water the plants. We have also created artifical islands in the lakes and amazing floating gardens.

6. CALENDARS
Our calendars are a wonder. One, the *xiuhpohualli*, has 365 days and describes the days and rituals according to the seasons. The other, the sacred calendar, or *tonalpohualli*, has 260 days showing time divided among the gods.

Submit Your Answer

SEE INSIDE:

Monty's Blog p. 27

REGULAR CONTRIBUTORS: Montezuma, Snake Woman, Hernán Cortés

Careers Guide pp. 8–9

Shopping Tips pp. 14–15

WELCOME TO
TENOCHTITLAN

Our capital city is the wonder of Mesoamerica. It stands on an island in Lake Texcoco, linked to the shore by long, gleaming causeways. With a population of 200,000, it is larger than any European city of our time. The pyramid temples are awesome! *HAIL!* guides you around town.

Why here?

Our god, Huitzilopochtli, told us to build where we found an eagle clutching a serpent, perched on a prickly-pear cactus. The name Tenochtitlan means "place of the prickly-pear cactus." It was not much at the time. We had to drain the marsh and build an aqueduct to bring fresh water. That made it more like home!

FINDING YOUR WAY

Tenochtitlan is divided into four districts: the Flowery Place, Heron's Home, Mosquito Fen, and Place of Gods. It is designed like a grid and divided by roads and canals. There's a humungous great square in the center with towering pyramids, so it is pretty hard to get lost.

FLOATING GARDENS

The island had little space for farming, so we had to build floating fields called *chinampas* to grow our food. We piled earth into a framework made of reeds, stamped it down, weighted it with stones, and presto, an instant field.

GREAT TEMPLE

The Great Temple is the tallest building in the city, about 100 feet (30 m) high. Very steep steps lead up to the top platform, which holds the temples of Huitzilopochtli and the rain god, Tlaloc. We sacrifice people daily here, and leave their heads to rot on enormous skull racks.

HEALTH WARNING!

Living in Tenochtitlan can seriously damage your health. The place is swarming with mosquitoes and poisonous spiders. The nearby volcanoes may erupt at any moment, and drought, famine, floods, and plagues of locusts are a constant threat.

TEMPLE SQUARE

Our central square has several temples. It is vast and surrounded by high walls. No commoners are allowed in, or foreigners for that matter. It is where we do our sacrifices, so watch your step if you take a peek.

TOP SIGHTS OUT OF TOWN

If you want to explore further afield, the city of Teotihuacan (above) is close. No one is sure who built it, but it is the largest city in Mesoamerica and is dominated by two massive pyramid temples. The city of Tula is not far away. This was built by the Toltecs but had been abandoned by the time we arrived.

CAREERS GUIDE

GREAT SPEAKER

The title of the Aztec emperor. You live in a palace and are waited on hand and foot by scores of servants. You are treated like a god and get to boss everyone around.

Qualifications: You must be high-born to get elected to this top post. It is really hard to break into as the new emperor is usually a close relative of the previous one.

SNAKE WOMAN

The emperor's deputy has a weird title, as he is always a man. You will be in charge of the day-to-day running of the empire. The pay is high, you do not pay tax, and you live in a house provided by the state. A key job.

Qualifications: Only leading noblemen may apply. It helps to be the emperor's younger brother.

PRIEST

Do not apply for the priesthood if you are fussy about hygiene. Priests hardly ever wash and have long, matted hair crawling with lice. Your clothes will always be blood-splattered from performing sacrifices and you will smell to high heaven. On the plus side you will be powerful, and you get free board and lodging.

Qualifications: Despite appearances, you need to be highborn and well-educated.

SOLDIER

A career with good prospects if you are handy with weapons. No pay, but brave deeds will win you riches and slaves. A commoner who captures four prisoners alive can become a nobleman.

Qualifications: Will suit those of a bloodthirsty nature.

There is plenty of work in the Aztec empire, but some jobs are more appealing than others. Our career expert guides you through the world of employment, with job descriptions and the qualifications needed.

SCRIBE

Scribes keep records such as taxes, accounts, and the history of the empire in books called codices that fold up like accordians. The Aztec script is pretty tricky—a system of picture writing that uses symbols called glyphs.

Qualifications: You need to be smart and well-educated.

PORTER

With no horses, carts, or roads, the job of porter is really bad news. It is fine if you don't mind slogging along rough tracks in bare feet, and lugging up to 90 lbs (40 kg) on your back.

Qualifications: None needed. Not recommended as a job, although you do see a bit of the world

MERCHANT

You get to travel and can also act as a government spy, which gives you a double income. Some merchants are filthy rich, but as a spy you are not allowed to show that you are rich, so you have to keep a low profile when in town.

Qualifications: A trade background is useful, but some start with nothing and work their way up.

FARMER

Aztec farmers work the land without metal tools, plows, carts, or horses to pull them. You break up earth using a wooden digging stick, and sow, weed, and harvest by hand. Oh, and you collect human waste from public toilets to fertilize the fields.

Qualifications: None needed, just blood, sweat, and tears

SLAVE

Bottom of the pile. You do all the dirty jobs for no pay, and run a high risk of being sacrificed.

Qualifications: No one is born a slave, but you could end up as one if you get caught committing a crime or avoiding taxes, or if you are captured in war.

What's On in
AZTEC TOWN?

★ ★ ★ ☆ ☆

DAILY SACRIFICE

Human sacrifices take place daily at sunset at the Great Temple. A priest cuts the victim's chest open, rips out the heart, and offers it to the gods. It is the only way to make sure that the Sun rises every day and the world will not end tomorrow, so it is all for a good cause. Take care—the steps of the temple are slippery with blood!

DIY SACRIFICE

The priest explains how to make the ultimate sacrifice.

1. Lead your victim up the temple steps and stretch him or her out on the sacrificial stone.
2. Get your fellow priests to hold the victim down while you open the chest with a flint knife.
3. Quickly cut out the beating heart and place it in the container provided, which is called a *chacmool*.
4. Toss the lifeless body down the steps and watch it bounce to the bottom.

Step right up!

" Cruel? Nonsense! Our gods insist on blood, and it is an honor to be sacrificed because you are sure of a happy life after death. The flint knife is very sharp, so you hardly feel a thing. The ideal victim is young, fit, and handsome—only the best for the gods! "

☆ ☆ ☆ ☆ ☆

Entertainment Aztec-style is not for the faint-hearted. It is mostly deadly serious, deeply religious—and positively gory. Aztecs are big on spectator sports, but it is better to watch, as participants usually end up dead. *HAIL!* has the latest on all the top events in town.

MY HEART'S ON FIRE

You are in for a rare treat if you catch the New Fire ceremony. It is only held once every 52 years to mark the start of the new calendar. A carefully selected victim is killed by setting fire to his heart while it is still in his body. Runners carry torches lit by the human bonfire to every part of the city.

IT'S SWINGTIME!

During festivals you can witness the dance of the *voladores*. Four youths dressed in bird costumes leap off a high pole. Dangling by ropes tied to their ankles, each spins round the pole 13 times. That is 52 spins in all— the same number as the years in the Aztec calendar. Do not try it if you get dizzy. You need a head for heights, too.

GAMBLING FOR HIGH STAKES

If gambling is your thing, you'll love *patolli*. It is an Aztec version of backgammon, with players rolling dice and moving counters around an X-shaped board. Stakes are high. Players bet their clothes, house, land, and even their children. If you lose, you could wind up a slave.

SACRED BALL GAME

In *tlachtli*, the Aztec version of basketball, two teams of noblemen compete to send a rubber ball through hoops set high above the ball court. The ball is solid rubber and you can only use your knees, hips, and elbows. The losers have to give the winners their clothes and possessions.

CELEBRITY

Our gods and goddesses are a scary bunch. We have to offer them blood sacrifices every day or they think we do not love them. Tloque Nahuaque, Lord of Nowhere, is the ultimate Big Brother. He has shut the other gods and goddesses in a temple. They must explain why they should win your vote.

QUETZALCOATL

Role: God of life, learning, rain, and wind
Appearance: Feathered serpent

> I created humankind, so you humans would not be here without me. I also sacrificed myself to help my people, so I am one of the good guys. Of course, I still like my daily sacrifice.

XILONEN

Role: Goddess of the corn

> I protect the maize crop. I'm genuinely kind and gentle, so I could win—if the other gods do not kill me!

TLALOC

Role: God of rain and lightning

> I make crops grow, but I can also send floods that will wreck the harvest. When there's a drought, you will need to sacrifice children to me.

Did you know?

There is a god for almost every aspect of life in the Aztec culture.

HUITZILOPOCHTLI

Role: God of war, the Sun, and Aztec emperors

> I'm the Aztecs' very own god. I showed them where to settle and build their capital city. I'm also handy in a scrap, with my magical weapon, the fire serpent.

BIG BROTHER

XOCHIPILLI

Role: Prince of flowers, god of dawn, poetry, love, and happiness
Appearance: Young man with the face of a corpse

> I'm god of dancing, gambling, and the ball game. I sound jolly, but like the other gods I am actually pretty menacing. In Aztec culture, even flowers are linked to death and sacrifice.

COATLICUE

Role: Earth goddess
Appearance: Terrifying, with huge clawed hands, a skirt made of living snakes, and a necklace of severed hands, hearts, and heads.

> I stand for death, poverty, and the harshness of life. I'm so hideous that when a European explorer dug up my statue, he quickly buried it again!

Did you know?
Coatlicue is the mother of Huitzilopochtli and his evil sister Coyolxauhqui, the goddess of the Moon. Coyolxauhqui tried to murder her mother.

TEZCATLIPOCA

Role: God of magic, war, and death, his name means "smoking mirror."

> I spend my life fighting with Quetzalcoatl. I am master of sorcery and can see everything in my magic mirror. I invented human sacrifice. I'm so scary that even the Aztecs are terrified of me.

SHOPPING TIPS

If shopping is your thing, look no further than the Aztec empire. Track down all the best bargains at the huge market in the nearby city of Tlatelolco. *HAIL!*'s top team of shopaholics are on hand to guide you around.

FINDING YOUR WAY AROUND

The market covers a huge area, so it is quite easy to get lost. Think of it as a collection of mini-markets, with different areas that specialize in grain, precious stones, building materials, fish, livestock, and fresh produce. Head for the craft area to buy jewelry, pots, featherwork, and carvings. Check out the livestock section to pick up a turkey or parrot for supper. You can get a haircut or a hot snack, have your fortune told, or catch up on the latest gossip.

WHEN AND WHERE?

Tlatelolco is just outside Tenochtitlan. The enormous market held there every five days attracts an amazing 50,000 people. Get there at dawn to see the merchants setting up shop. By eight a.m. the market is in full swing. The shouts of the traders can be heard three miles (five km) away!

SHOPPING HEAVEN

" We interview a housewife heading for the market.

If you asked me to choose between going to heaven or to the market, I'd choose heaven, of course. But I'd like a quick trip to the market first!

GET YOUR LUCKY CHARMS HERE

A shady dealer draws us aside and opens his sack.

"You will never guess what is in here—the hair and fingers of women who have died in childbirth! I said you wouldn't guess. Warriors see these things as lucky charms—they stick them on their shields for protection in battle. And where do I find them? Let's just say I visit the graveyard at night and ambush the odd funeral procession. Ah, excuse me, I must be going, I see an official coming."

DIRTY DEALS

Watch out for fakers and cheats at the market. Sneaky merchants sell moldy chilies or try to pass off cactus-fiber cloth as fine cotton. Fakers make false cacao beans by stuffing bean husks with sawdust. Luckily, officials are on hand to make sure prices are fair and no one gets ripped off.

Buy or barter?

Aztecs do not actually use money—we use cacao beans instead. You can also exchange copper bars or cotton cloaks for small items. If you are paying out you will need gold grains, which come stored in handy quills of different sizes. Of course, you can also lug your own wares to market and swap for what you want.

FINEST FEATHERWORK

Come buy our fine feather cloaks, shields, and headdresses. Each is a masterpiece of small feathers, dyed with natural materials such as squashed insects. We are a family business—women dye and sort the feathers, men cut the cloth and stick on the feathers, and the kids make glue from bat poo.

FOR SALE

WELCOME TO MY BEAUTIFUL HOME!

Aztec palaces are built on a lavish scale with all the latest modern conveniences. Most of us live in less spectacular homes. *HAIL!*'s reporter tours the mansions of the high and mighty, and sneaks a peek into more humble abodes.

ENTERTAINING THE EMPEROR

The Great Speaker likes to be entertained at banquets. Musicians perform on drums, flutes, and whistles. If they sing out of tune or play a wrong note they are executed. Clowns and jugglers also perform—the same penalty applies if they tell an unfunny joke or drop a ball.

FIT FOR THE EMPEROR

A courtier shows us around the emperor's palace in Tenochtitlan.

"You need a guide to find your way around this place. It is large—a maze of courtyards, passages, staterooms, and guest rooms. There are several libraries, a court, workshops, and even a dungeon if you displease the emperor. The largest meeting hall can seat 3,000 people. The Great Speaker sees 600 visitors a day—mostly ambassadors and foreign gentry. You could wander all day and still not see it all. The grounds are vast, too. We lost one visitor for a week!"

Imperial Zoo

His highness Montezuma II has established a private zoo. It includes an aviary with ten rooms of rare birds, and a splendid collection of pumas and jaguars. The royal rattlesnakes live in jars lined with feathers. There are no records of living subjects being fed to the animals, but knowing the emperor, I could not say for sure.

PALACE RATIONS

We interview the head chef in the palace kitchens

" We feed about 2,000 people a day here, what with all the visiting noblemen and their servants. That's an awful lot of food. We get through 20,000 tortillas, 40 baskets of chilies, ten baskets of tomatoes, 100 turkeys, and 300 lbs (140 kg) of beans—and that's just the appetizers for one day. "

WELCOME TO MY HUMBLE HOME...

A commoner shows us around his hovel.

" Do come in. It's small, but commoners are forbidden to build two-storey houses. Just two rooms for 15 of us, but at least we don't have much furniture—only a few mats, baskets, and cooking pots. Go through into the shared courtyard. The women do all the cooking, spinning, and weaving here.

What's in Your FRIDGE?

Aztecs love home cooking. Many of our recipes will still be served up all over Mexico hundreds of years from now. *HAIL!*'s food team explain how to eat, drink, and be merry Aztec-style.

WHAT'S COOKING?

Maize (corn) is the Aztec staple. It is ground into flour and baked to make crispy *tortillas*, or stuffed with beans and vegetables and steamed gently. Veggies feature high on the menu, with stews made of squash, sweet potatoes, tomatoes, leeks, artichokes, and cactus leaves. Protein? It all depends on what the hunters bring back. You might get turkey, rabbit, deer, or armadillo if you are lucky. And frog, monkey, parrot, owl, or lizard if you are not. Eggs are a delicacy.

OUR NUTRITIONIST SAYS...

The Aztec diet is pretty healthy. There are no cattle, which means no fatty milk, cheese, or butter to raise your cholesterol level. There's no sugar either, so honey is used to sweeten foods. Poor people live on maize, beans, and veggies seven days a week. Even rich people don't eat much meat.

HOW HUNGRY ARE YOU?
1505 CE

The Aztec empire has been struck by famine. As food stocks run low, people are eating whatever they can find—seeds, snakes, cactus fruit, grasshoppers, and tadpoles. They are so desperate that boys are even scooping green scum off the lake and molding it into cakes.

Spice It Up!

We like our food good and spicy. We use red-hot chilies in almost every dish, including hot chocolate. But it is a fine line between pain and pleasure. We also use chilies in medicines and punishments!

AND TO DRINK?

Aztec beer is made from chewed maize. Mmm! A strong liquor called *pulque* is made from the sap of the maguey cactus. But only people over the age of 40 are allowed to drink alcohol. If you get caught for underage drinking, you may have your head shaved if you are a commoner. If you are noble, the punishment is death!

SERIOUSLY HOT CHOCOLATE

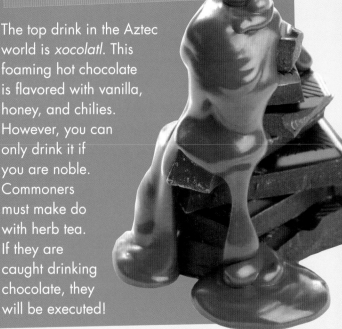

The top drink in the Aztec world is *xocolatl*. This foaming hot chocolate is flavored with vanilla, honey, and chilies. However, you can only drink it if you are noble. Commoners must make do with herb tea. If they are caught drinking chocolate, they will be executed!

STEWED POOCH!

We Aztecs love tasty dog casserole. We rear a special breed of hairless dog called a chihuahua just for the purpose. Your pampered pooch grows up in the home and is treated like a family member until it is time to slit its throat and pop it in the pot.

GOOD MANNERS

Dos and don'ts at banquets

1. Don't eat too fast or smack your lips while you are eating.

2. Don't sneeze or spit on your neighbor's food.

3. Try not to spill food down other people's clothes—it is OK to mess up your own.

STYLE FILE

A word of warning—an Aztec's clothes show his or her position in society. It is strictly against the law to wear clothes that are above your station. The first time you are caught for this crime, your house could be knocked down. For a second offense, the penalty is death.

OFFICIAL DRESS CODE

by order of the emperor

Our dress code is perfectly straightforward:

WOMEN: Wear a blouse and ankle-length skirt. No new fashions.

MEN: Commoners wear a loincloth and short cloak, knotted at the shoulder. Nobles are allowed to wear a long cloak and tunic. A long cloak is also allowed for warriors who have horrid battle scars on their legs.

CHOOSE THE RIGHT CLOTH: Commoners are only allowed garments made of scratchy cactus fiber. Nobles may wear soft, comfortable cotton.

DECORATION: Ordinary people's garments may have a patterned border. Nobles—you are allowed to wear hand-embroidered clothes sewn with gold thread and stitched with jewels or feathers.

SEVERE punishments for breaking the rules!

AZTEC BLING

Jewelry? Sure, but similar rules apply as with clothing. Ordinary people may wear jewelry made of shells or polished stones. Commoners are forbidden to carry flowers or fans—on pain of death. Well-to-do people wear as much rich jewelry as possible to show their status. Heavy necklaces, bangles, earrings, lip plugs made of solid gold encrusted with jewels…it may not be comfortable, but at least it's showy!

HAIRSTYLES

Strict rules apply to hairstyles to show your class and marital status.

YOUNG GIRLS: Wear your hair long and loose to show you are a maiden.

MARRIED WOMEN: Braid your hair and knot it in two horns above your forehead. Very attractive!

BOYS: Wear your hair loose and long until you have killed or captured your first prisoner. Your long hair shows you are not a "real man" yet, and avoid calling anyone "Tufty" as it is an official insult.

WARRIORS: You are allowed to cut your hair short and tie it in a topknot.

Skin Problems?

✪ If you discover you have **fleas**, smear the affected areas with a layer of pine resin (tree sap) and set it on fire. This will deal with the fleas, but you may have third-degree burns!

✪ **Nasty rash**? Smear the affected area with the sap from a squashed cactus. Remove the spines first or the rash could get worse.

Did you know?

The Aztecs liked to dye their clothes with bright colors. They made a red dye from the cochineal beetle. It took about 70,000 beetles to make 1 lb (0.5 kg) of the dye.

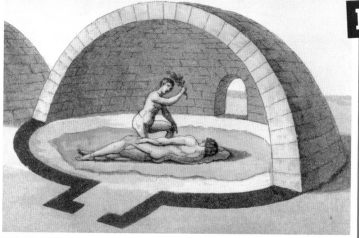

KEEPING CLEAN

Aztecs like to be clean, tidy, and well scrubbed (except priests, that is). Many families have a bathhouse in the garden that works like a sauna. A fire is lit outside to heat the mudbrick walls. Then water is thrown inside to create steam. You enter, steam gently, and beat your skin with a bunch of twigs to get it squeaky clean.

EDUCATION SUPPLEMENT:
GROWING UP

We Aztecs love our children—of course we do. It is just that we believe that training should start early, if we are to mold the little dears into model citizens. Our expert guides you through the minefield of Aztec education.

FOOD ALLOWANCE

Children's food is to be carefully rationed according to age. Children aged 11 and 12 are allowed one and a half *tortillas* plus vegetables each day. Kids of 13 and 14 are allowed two *tortillas* plus vegetables, but no second helpings!

BY LAW!

WELCOME, CHILD!

Aztec life is no bowl of cherries. The sooner our kids know it, the better! That is why we greet every newborn baby with these words: "Welcome to a place of pain and torment, where it is always either too hot or too cold. You will be ill and exhausted. You will go thirsty and hungry." Babies may not understand immediately, but they will when they grow!

SCHOOL

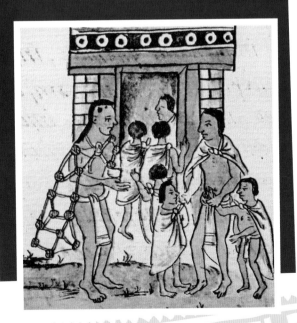

At 15, all boys start school. Most kids go to the *telpochcalli* or youth house. They learn a bit of history and religion, but mostly practical skills, such as fighting, farming, digging ditches, and mending temples. Noble boys go to *calmecac*, or temple school, where they train to be administrators, priests, and warriors. They learn to read and write, and study religion, history, warfare, astronomy, and poetry. Girls mostly learn at home, though well-off girls may be trained in temple duties.

THE EMPIRE EXPECTS...

Aztec society has strict rules on the duties that children are expected to perform at every age.

⚙ **GIRLS** aged four know how to spin. By 12, your duties will include sweeping the floor, making bread, cooking, and weaving (left). Between 12 and 15, you will probably marry and go to live in your husband's home.

⚙ **BOYS** aged four are expected to fetch water and carry firewood. At six, you will work in the fields, fish, and take goods to market. At 13, you should be able to paddle a dugout canoe (right) —quite tricky to do!

DOs AND DON'Ts FOR CHILDREN

⚙ **Don't set a bad example by interrupting when you are spoken to. Keep your answers short and sensible.**

⚙ **Don't make faces or rude gestures (however much you might want to).**

⚙ **All children are expected to be helpful, work incredibly hard, and to top it all off, look cheerful at all times! Look on the bright side—one day you will be grown up and have kids of your own to boss around.**

BEHAVE—OR ELSE!

If children do not pay attention, they are pricked with cactus spines. If they misbehave, they are stripped naked, tied hand and foot, and left in a puddle all night! For disobedience, they are held over a fire of hot chili peppers with their head in the choking smoke.

SOLD INTO SLAVERY!

HAIL! has discovered that Aztecs who are very hard-up are selling their kids into slavery. It sounds pretty mean, but in fact there is a good chance that they will be better treated by their new masters than they were at home. They will be expected to work night and day, but then, for them that is normal.

BREAKING NEWS!

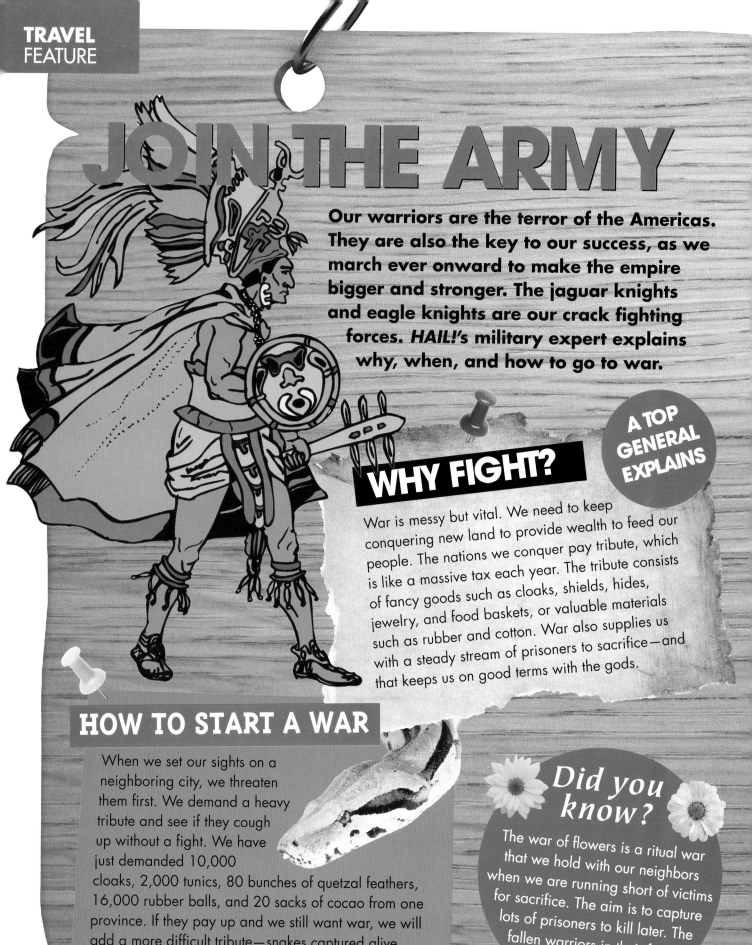

JOIN THE ARMY

Our warriors are the terror of the Americas. They are also the key to our success, as we march ever onward to make the empire bigger and stronger. The jaguar knights and eagle knights are our crack fighting forces. *HAIL!*'s military expert explains why, when, and how to go to war.

A TOP GENERAL EXPLAINS

WHY FIGHT?

War is messy but vital. We need to keep conquering new land to provide wealth to feed our people. The nations we conquer pay tribute, which is like a massive tax each year. The tribute consists of fancy goods such as cloaks, shields, hides, jewelry, and food baskets, or valuable materials such as rubber and cotton. War also supplies us with a steady stream of prisoners to sacrifice—and that keeps us on good terms with the gods.

HOW TO START A WAR

When we set our sights on a neighboring city, we threaten them first. We demand a heavy tribute and see if they cough up without a fight. We have just demanded 10,000 cloaks, 2,000 tunics, 80 bunches of quetzal feathers, 16,000 rubber balls, and 20 sacks of cocao from one province. If they pay up and we still want war, we will add a more difficult tribute—snakes captured alive.

Did you know?

The war of flowers is a ritual war that we hold with our neighbors when we are running short of victims for sacrifice. The aim is to capture lots of prisoners to kill later. The fallen warriors in their finery look like pretty petals.

SEE THE WORLD

MILITARY OUTFITTERS
BY ORDER OF THE EMPEROR

Everything you need for battle:

WEAPONS—Clubs and swords studded with razor-sharp flakes of obsidian that will slice an enemy's ear off cleanly. Spears tipped with obsidian, supplied with a spear-thrower to make your aim go further. Bows and slings complete with pebble ammunition.

ARMOR of quilted cotton soaked in salty water and dried to set rock-hard.

FINERY for officers: animal skins, eagle claws and feathers, flags, and standards.

TREATMENT OF PRISONERS
DOs AND DON'Ts FOR WARRIORS

DO feed your prisoners well and treat them like members of your family until it's time to sacrifice them at the temple.

DON'T eat your own prisoners. It is bad manners. You may be invited to eat a tasty stew made from the limbs of other people's prisoners. If so, you should accept politely—it is delicious.

DON'T eat any parts of prisoners apart from the arms and legs. The other parts are fed to animals in the zoo.

THE JAGUAR KNIGHTS

Join the elite force of the Aztec empire. We take young men straight from school and mold them into soldiers. Warriors that capture three prisoners alive become full knights, with a jaguar skin complete with the snarling head as helmet. We initiate our warriors by smearing their faces with the blood from a still-beating human heart.

HUNK OF THE MONTH

Our emperor, Montezuma II, is a great warrior. Elected from the top nobles, he is treated as a god. Unfortunately, he is also a wee bit superstitious, which may prove his undoing.

COURT ETIQUETTE
HOW TO BEHAVE IN THE PRESENCE OF THE EMPEROR

✓ Nobles must remove cloaks and sandals in the presence of the Great Speaker.

✓ If he addresses you, answer: "Lord, O my great lord."

✗ It is strictly forbidden to look the *tlatoani* (the emperor) in the eye. Keep your head bowed and your eyes on the ground.

✗ It is forbidden to turn your back on the emperor, so you have to walk out backward—watch out for the furniture!

CELEBRITY INTERVIEW: MONTEZUMA II

Profile: Born in 1466, Montezuma was brought up in the palace and schooled at the *calmecac*. At the age of 20, he married his first wife. He was elected Great Speaker in 1502, having proved his bravery in battle.

Q *Lord, O my great lord, what do you like most about your job?*

A I get carried around in a litter. When I step down, my nobles spread their cloaks before me. It's a great feeling!

Q *It's 1517 – you've been in power for 15 years now. What are your greatest achievements?*

A I've won many great victories but I haven't defeated all our neighbors yet.

Did you know?
Montezuma is also known as Moctezuma or Motecuhzoma.

MONTY'S BLOG

In 1519, a small force of Spanish soldiers led by Hernán Cortés landed in Mexico in search of treasure. The Aztecs had never seen white men before, let alone soldiers in metal armor with horses, guns, and cannons. They mistook the Spanish for gods—a big mistake, as Montezuma's blog reveals.

November 1518 My empire is the mightiest it's ever been, but lately we've had a string of bad omens. Flaming stars, burning temples...it reminds me of the legend of Quetzalcoatl. They say the mighty god was driven from this land, but will one day return to claim it. He will have a pale face and a beard. What's more, the world will end soon after! I can't stop thinking about it and I'm losing my beauty sleep.

March 1519 Messengers have arrived bringing news of godlike strangers on the coast. Apparently they arrived in a huge floating house...they ride four-legged monsters and have metal skin! And their weapons spit fire! And guess what, they've got pale faces with beards—it looks like Quetzalcoatl has returned!

May 1519 My spies say the men-gods are heading toward us. I'm sending gifts and a stern warning to try to head them off. Hope it works.

November 1519 My plan failed, and the strangers have arrived. It's no good skulking in my palace any longer. I've decided to put on my finery and go out to meet them. If it is Quetzalcoatl I'll have to hand over my empire. Hopefully they'll be so dazzled by me they won't try to take over. Fingers crossed.

UNDER NEW MANAGEMENT
THE SPANISH CONQUEST

CELEB PROFILE: HERNÁN CORTÉS

Born in Spain in 1485. In 1504, he sailed for Hispaniola (Cuba) to seek his fortune. The island had been discovered just 11 years earlier by one Christopher Columbus. In Hispaniola, Cortés heard rumors of a fabulously wealthy empire on the mainland. He managed to get himself put in charge of an expedition to bring back treasure.

HERNAN'S BLOG

March 1519 We've arrived! Five hundred men, horses, and cannons all landed safely. I've burned my ships to show the men there's no turning back!

May 1519 Apparently, the wealthy empire inland is ruled by a people called the Aztecs. The people around here hate them. I've recruited a local woman, Dona Marina, who speaks Spanish to persuade the locals to join us.

In 1518, Montezuma ruled an empire that stretched right across Mexico. Just three years later, the emperor was dead, and his empire lay in the hands of the Spanish. How did it happen? *HAIL!* is able to reveal the sensational story, thanks to the blog of Spanish general Hernán Cortés.

August 1519 We're heading for the Aztec capital through the mountains. We've got an army of local people with us. They didn't need much persuasion to join our side!

November 1519 We've reached the city on the lake at last. It's as amazing as they said—an island city with soaring temples, surrounded by floating fields.

Next day The emperor, Montezuma, came out to meet us as we headed into town. Seems to be mixing me up with someone called Quetzalcoatl. He has invited us to stay in one of his palaces. The Aztecs seem amazingly advanced, apart from the human sacrifices. But we're still going to steal their treasure.

Soon after Success! We managed to capture Montezuma as we entered the royal palace. Now we've taken over the palace and Monty is a prisoner.

yeçtla ti tetzavitl yn mal ques.

July 1520 I was away on business and my men panicked during a festival and killed a lot of nobles. I rushed back and ordered Monty to calm his people. But they threw stones at him—one hit him on the head and that was the end of him. An Aztec army ambushed us, slaughtered my men, and I barely escaped with my life.

March 1521 I swore I'd be back one day and now I am, with a huge army of local people. We've surrounded Tenochtitlan and we're going to starve them out.

August 1521 Victory! We conquered the city. We've flattened most of it and slaughtered thousands of Aztecs just to be on the safe side. Now the Aztec empire is a colony of Spain and I'm going to be governor. We ship out the treasure next week!

STOP PRESS!

....

The Spanish didn't have it all their own way. Many of the treasure ships were sunk or captured by pirates on their way to Spain. Hernán Cortés fell out of favor and died forgotten in 1547. After 300 years of Spanish rule, Mexico achieved independence.

GLOSSARY

aviary A large cage or enclosure in which birds are kept

barter Negotiate the trading of goods without the exchange of money

calmecac A temple school for the education of the children of Aztec nobility

captive A person who is held prisoner

causeway A raised road or path across water or marshland

chacmool A statue used to hold the blood of sacrificial victims

chinampas The "floating gardens" of the Aztecs, a method of farming using rectangle-shaped floating islands to grow crops

codices (*singular* codex) The picture books that recorded the lives of the Aztecs

corpse A dead body, usually of a human

courtier A servant in a royal court

famine Widespread hunger and starvation

gentry People of noble birth or high position

glyph A picture symbol, used in Aztec writing

litter A chair suspended between shafts and carried by people

obsidian A hard, glassy volcanic stone

omen A sign, believed to warn of a future good or evil event

patolli An Aztec board game

pulque An alcoholic drink made from the sap of the maguey cactus

quill The hollow part of a bird's feather

scribe A professional writer

standard A military emblem

tlachtli The sacred ball game of the Aztecs, also played by the Mayans, in which the aim is to put a ball through a hoop made of stone

tlatoani The "Great Speaker" or Aztec emperor

tortilla A maize (corn) pancake

tribute An enforced gift, like a kind of tax

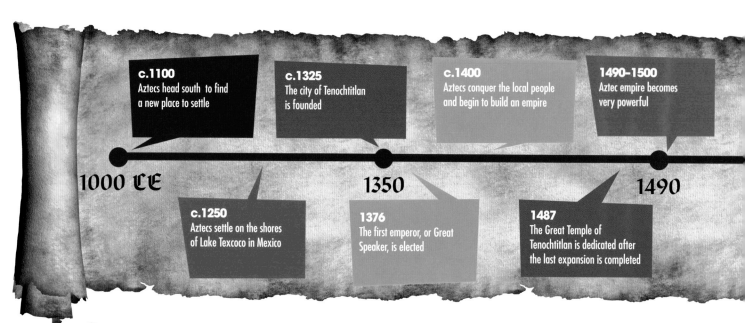

c.1100 Aztecs head south to find a new place to settle

c.1325 The city of Tenochtitlan is founded

c.1400 Aztecs conquer the local people and begin to build an empire

1490–1500 Aztec empire becomes very powerful

1000 CE

1350

1490

c.1250 Aztecs settle on the shores of Lake Texcoco in Mexico

1376 The first emperor, or Great Speaker, is elected

1487 The Great Temple of Tenochtitlan is dedicated after the last expansion is completed

ON THE INTERNET

A site with sections on every aspect of Aztec life, including gods, food, sports and games, school, dress, farming, trade, and medicine
http://library.thinkquest.org/27981/

Map of the Aztec empire, creation myths, the Aztec calendar, and life in Mesoamerica
www.crystalinks.com/aztecs.html

All about Aztec musical instruments and music—listen to the sounds made by copies of the skull-shaped whistle or the large horned toad-shaped ocarina
**www.mexicolore.co.uk/index.php?
one=azt&two=mus**

The gods of Aztec mythology, their appearance, their history, and their powers
**www.godchecker.com/pantheon/aztec-
mythology.php**

Aztec history, Aztec religious beliefs, and the significance of the different types of sacrifice
**www.aztec-history.com/aztec-
sacrifice.html**

A site about the amazing temples and pyramids built by the Aztecs
www.aztec-history.net/aztec_temples

Aztec calendars and how to read them, the Sun stone, and Aztec cosmology
www.azteccalendar.com/

BOOKS

Life of the Ancient Aztecx (Peoples of the Ancient World) by Lynn Peppas (Crabtree Publishing, 2004)

The Aztec Empire by Jane Bingham (Harcourt Education, 2007)

The Facts About the Aztecs by Jen Green (Wayland, 2007)

Eyewitness Aztec (Dorling Kindersley, 2006)

Aztec: Kids at the Crossroad by Laura Scandiffio and Tina Holdcroft (Annick Press, 2009)

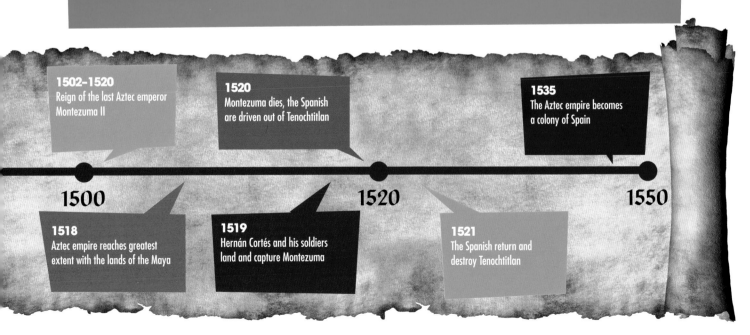

1502–1520
Reign of the last Aztec emperor Montezuma II

1520
Montezuma dies, the Spanish are driven out of Tenochtitlan

1535
The Aztec empire becomes a colony of Spain

1500

1520

1550

1518
Aztec empire reaches greatest extent with the lands of the Maya

1519
Hernán Cortés and his soldiers land and capture Montezuma

1521
The Spanish return and destroy Tenochtitlan

INDEX